the little book of

BONSAI

matthew puntigam

photography by jonathan hökklo

Hardie Grant

QUADRILLE

CONTENTS

INTRODUCTION

WHAT IS BONSAI?

In its simplest form, bonsai is the art of caring for trees. The Japanese and Chinese characters for bonsai roughly translate to 'potted plant', and records indicate this form of plant care was widely practised by the wealthy and privileged nobles in the 16th century. By the 19th century, the art form had taken root among a wider populace, and bonsai adorned the homes and gardens of Japanese merchants at a time when trees were widely accepted as sacred - especially in the animist Shintó tradition. Over the last century bonsai has spread from Japan and China quickly and continues to gain popularity all over the world.

So, you may ask, 'If a bonsai is just a potted plant, aren't all my house plants bonsai now?' Before you start thinking that you were a bonsai master all along, remember the difference lies in care and maintenance. Bonsai is a style of plant care, developed into an art form, in which trees, usually 1m (3ft) or less in height, are shaped and styled into small representations of larger scenes found in nature. Some of those shapes have names like 'windswept' or 'cascading', and the scenes they depict might represent a mountainside, valley, or even a sandy beach. Think of bonsai as a form of plant parenting taken to the next level. Instead of adding water and nervously hoping your plant will grow, you're really paying attention to their needs and planning for their long-term wellbeing. You'll pair them

with the best location around the house, match them with the appropriate tools to help their success, make sure they are getting the best nutrients, and maybe even ornament them with cute accessories so they really feel special.

This book is for anyone who is interested in getting started; maybe you've been given a bonsai as a gift or are about to give one. You might have a few already and are finally ready to grow your collection. It covers all of the basics to set you on a firm path, which you can explore as far as you'd like.

HOW TO USE THIS BOOK
Each entry includes key information about caring for that particular plant. All the information is clearly organised under appropriate symbols which will help you give your plants everything they need to grow and thrive.

KEY TO SYMBOLS

✂ STYLING   ° TEMPERATURE

❋ LIGHT   ⠿ SOIL

◐ WATER   🪰 PESTS

Each plant is given its scientific and common names; occasionally these are the same. Common names vary greatly across regions, requiring the use of a formal naming system. The scientific name consists of two words: the genus and the species, and provides information about the relationship between plants. Cultivars, written in single quotes, are different varieties of the same species, selected artificially for particular traits. Often, tree cultivars are clones, guaranteeing the same defining characteristics for that cultivar each time.

THE BENEFITS OF COLLECTING BONSAI

Bonsai is about storytelling; it appeals to our ability to communicate through metaphor and connect with a living object on an intimate level. If you've experienced that moment when you forget your worries while walking through woods, you'll understand the healing power of trees. Forest walks are increasingly part of the discussion about the therapeutic effects of nature on stress and anxiety. It is nothing new; the Japanese term *shin-rin-yoku* means forest bathing and refers to visiting woods for clarity and cleansing. Although one tree might not be a substitute for the biodiversity of a forest, the mental capacity to focus on each leaf and branch of a bonsai tree can recharge your focus and transport you far from home; your imagination recreates the forest and your physiology believes it. This is how I came to enjoy bonsai: as a meditative and healing art. Working with living material to create something beautiful is an act of kindness and interacting with bonsai brings a deep connection with the woods.

By design, trees are giving. They are nature's lungs, helping to purify the air and regulate temperature and humidity, and are irreplaceable in many other ways; an oak tree, for example, provides food and harbour for dozens of creatures. Studies show all house plants can improve the air quality of a home and, as living art, displaying bonsai brings a level of beauty that is hard to recreate with other objects. A well-placed bonsai is a place to rest the eyes and mind, whether alone or with others. Raising bonsai at home is a way to slow down and enjoy all of these beneficial side effects.

TOOLS AND EQUIPMENT

As a bonsai beginner you can start with basic tools like scissors or pruning shears, but as you advance there are specialized tools for a variety of tasks. Here are some of the most frequently used tools.

PRUNING TOOLS

- Bonsai scissors have a pointed tip and two cutting blades with a rounded bevel, best used on leaves and small branch pruning.
- Branch cutters will provide more bite and leverage on larger branches, making a cleaner cut.
- Knob cutters are best for removing branches near the trunk; they have a concave blade to create a pocket wound that heals faster by allowing bark to callous over easily.

REPOTTING TOOLS

- A repotting knife will help remove pot-bound material from planters by separating the roots from the planter sides; the flexible blade follows the planter contour, which is especially great for rounded pots.
- Root hooks help to loosen and open any tightly bound roots.
- Root picks do the same and also help to work new soil into the root system. Metal root picks last longer than wooden, and taper to a point to help part roots when digging.
- Wire or plastic mesh covers drainage holes to stop soil from falling out after watering.
- Soil scoops allow you to measure out the soil mix and make it easier to direct the soil into small spaces and corners.

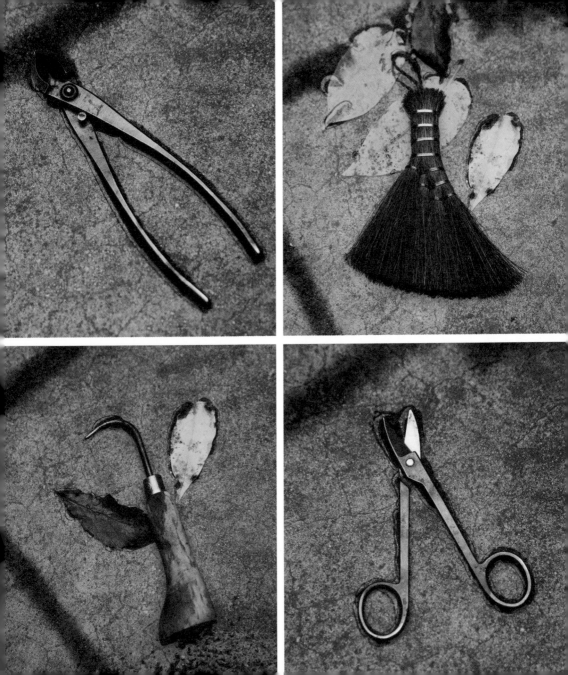

WATERING AND CLEANING TOOLS

- A spray bottle with an adjustable nozzle and pendulum dip tube, is best for misting and cleaning leaves and delicate plants like moss. They can be used upside down to spray up into the core of the plant, and the long metal nozzle adds pinpoint accuracy.
- A Watering can with a shower head that produces fine droplets will deliver a soft stream of water slow enough to soak in gently.
- Tweezers with a serrated grip point are used to pick out unwanted material from the tree or soil surface; the spatula end can be used to tamper and smooth out surfaces.
- A coconut fibre brush to keep tools and work areas clean of debris.

WIRING

- Wire comes in many sizes, the largest of which is only used for bending hardened older branches. For beginners common gauges will be 2.5mm (10), 2mm (12), 1.5mm (14), and 1mm (18), with lowest mm dimension (highest AWG number) denoting thinner wires that are more pliable. Copper or aluminium is most commonly used.
- Japanese wire cutters have a longer handle compared to standard cutters, and a rounded nose that allows you to get very close to branches without damaging them.
- Jin pliers have a serrated grip and are used to grab and move wire into position, sometimes more easily than with hands alone. They can also be used to create deadwood by removing pieces of bark or trunk in a styling technique called jin or shari.

PLANTERS

Planters are traditionally square or rectangular, but also come in round and oval shapes. Materials vary from glazed stoneware to porcelain, or even glass. All planters must have drainage holes large enough for an unimpeded flow of water and fast drainage, and a flat base so water doesn't pool in any areas. If the base is irregular, the drainage hole should be at the lowest point. A planter foot will raise the drainage hole and add airflow to the base of the pot, helping to prevent mould build up. Choose a size that will balance out the height and shape of your bonsai, increasing its perceived size and calling attention to the base of the trunk. The planter should not dominate the bonsai; a common rule is that it should be no more than one third the overall height of the bonsai. Quality planters will withstand many seasons of winter freezing if kept outdoors.

SOILS

Soil is responsible for holding your tree in place and providing the necessary environment for healthy nutrient exchange. A good soil will not stay soggy-wet too long, maintain its structure over time, and allow pockets of air for healthy root development. Fine particles should be sifted out before mixing to prevent caking or compacting at the bottom of the pot that could impede drainage. Trees can grow in a wide variety of substrates, but common bonsai mixes might include one or more of the following: peat, compost, fir or pine bark, horticultural charcoal, crushed stone, lava rock, calcined clay. It is best to experiment to find a composition that works best in your climate according to the yearly temperatures, humidity levels and type of bonsai. Organic soils like peat moss will hold water, like a sponge, and stay wet longer than inorganic soils like rocks and fired clay. A 40/60 mix of organic to inorganic would be suitable for tropical and humidity-loving plants, while a 20/80 mix would be better for outdoor pines, which need excellent drainage. For most bonsai, a good particle size is 3–5mm ($\frac{1}{8}$–$\frac{1}{4}$in).

BASIC BONSAI CARE

Beginner bonsai are not that different from other plants, and anyone can learn how to keep them alive successfully. First, establish if your bonsai is indoor or outdoor; this depends on where you live. Most bonsai in this book are species native to the tropics or subtropics, where they do fine outdoors in temperatures that usually stay above 10°C (50°F) year round. When kept in temperate zones, including most of the United States, Europe, and Northern Asia, these bonsai species will not survive outside through the colder winters, and in these zones they would be classified as *indoor*. Species native to temperate zones naturally overwinter outdoors and need temperatures below 10°C (50°F) to induce dormancy as part of their yearly cycle. We call these species *outdoor*. Look out the window and you might see good examples: maples, pines, and birches to name a few. If kept indoors in warm temperatures during winter they will eventually tire themselves, leading to a weakened immune system that can expose them to pests or disease.

WATERING
No plant can survive without this and it is also the most important part of bonsai care. Proper watering means getting water evenly distributed throughout the planter, so that every root has access to moisture. There are two types of watering: top watering and bottom watering. To bottom water, place your pot in a bowl of water, letting the planter soak up water through the drainage hole at the base. Submerge at least three-quarters of the planter for a minimum of 5 minutes;

alternatively you can submerge the entire pot, carefully making sure that the top dressing or moss remains undisturbed. Submerging ensures that all parts of the root system get wet. Top watering is done with a watering can, or gentle shower setting on any hose nozzle. When top-watering, water deeply and thoroughly until you see water exit the drainage hole. A hasty watering to one side of the pot might result in no water reaching drier areas on the other side.

Water when necessary; start with a regular weekly schedule and adjust appropriately according to the changing climate. Remember that smaller pots and shallow, wide pots dry out quickest, whereas taller or barrel shaped pots with narrow openings hold moisture longer. Your planter should drain quickly, and not puddle at the top (a sign of blocked or poor drainage). The rate at which your planter will dry out depends on humidity, heat, soil composition, type of plant, and the growing stage. Most plants suffer fatally if they dry out completely, especially during an active growing stage. It is a good idea to pick up your planter regularly and get a feel for how heavy it is when recently watered; if you mistakenly let your soil go bone-dry, you'll immediately know that it is too light.

LIGHT
Proper placement of the bonsai ensures it is getting the right amount of light to flourish, has proper ventilation, and maintains the right moisture levels. Always check the conditions appropriate for a particular bonsai and make small changes as necessary, moving or

placing blinds to control the amount of light throughout the year. With indoor environments, windows offer a variety of light conditions. In the northern hemisphere a northern-facing window typically gets little direct sunlight; an eastern-facing window provides a gentle but direct morning light; and a southern- and western-facing window will get the strongest light. The key is to match the appropriate tree to the conditions you can provide. Light levels can make the difference between a plant merely surviving, and fully thriving. Putting out new growth and blooming are activities that require a lot of energy; if your bonsai is meant to flower, light levels could play a factor. It is fine to move your bonsai around if necessary, as long as changes are gradual.

PRUNING

If left alone without guidance your bonsai will eventually lose its shape and become shrubby due to new growth. Pruning helps to maintain the shape by controlling direction and growth, strengthening, and preventing the bonsai from using soil resources too quickly. During the growing months of spring and summer, your tree could explode with new shoots that will need to be pruned back several times until the previous profile is achieved. With pruning shears or branch cutters, cut back the new growth, leaving one or two newer leaves, usually lighter in colour. Pruning styles will depend on the style of planting, but generally three simple rules dictate which branches should be removed: shoots that stick straight up, shoots that grow straight down, and shoots that grow back into the core of the tree thereby crossing other branches. These unruly shoots will quickly turn a sharp tree back into a hard-to-read bush and should be tamed.

WIRING

Learning how to style is not difficult, and results can be immediate, but with time comes a deeper understanding and appreciation for what makes some bonsai world class specimens and why. Connoisseurs may only consider finished bonsai worthy, but there are quicker ways to achieve characterful looks in only months or a few years. Copper wire is preferred by bonsai professionals due to the natural way it weathers and its ability to get stronger with bending, holding the branch shape. Some say it also repels pests such as slugs and snails. Aluminium is a cheaper alternative but works as well in most cases.

Get familiar with the flexibility of the wire and test any branches before wiring to determine the appropriate gauge. Already brittle branches may not be suitable for wiring and could break. New shoots and young saplings will be very pliable, rendering a heavier gauge unnecessary. As a beginner, test your wiring on less important branches or starter plants before moving on to more prominent ones. Cut a piece of wire about 1.5 times the length of the section to be wired, and start at the base of the branch. With one hand holding the base, wind at 45 degree angles to the branch as you make your way to the tip. With each rotation, reposition your hand to hold the area just wired for stability and control. Leave the wire slightly loose to allow for growth; if it's wound too tight, the wire will cut into the tree and will need to be removed sooner than expected.

If starting from the base of the trunk, firmly sink one end of the wire into the soil next to the base for stability and work up the trunk in the same way. Once you have wired and bent branches into position it is best not to continually readjust while the branches are hardening off

into their new shape. Check every few weeks to see that the wire is not damaging the trunk or branches, and after a growing season remove the wire by cutting it away or carefully reversing the process. If the branch bounces back into its original position, it will need to be rewired for a longer time.

FERTILIZER

Over time the nutrients and trace elements in soil will leach out after repeated watering and will need to be replaced. Signs of nutrient deficiency are lacklustre appearance and poor growth. Fertilizing at the right time and under the right concentration is important to avoid burning the tree or making a sick tree worse. Fertilize trees that are stable and look healthy; generally trees that are going through shock or recovering from a bug infestation are not heavily fertilized as this could shock their system further.

Fertilizers come in liquid forms, as water-soluble powders, or as slow-release pellets or granules. Liquid fertilizers are applied either by spray or watering can to the surface of the soil after a normal watering routine. Slow-release fertilizers are sprinkled on the soil surface or held in place by fertilizer baskets. These release fertilizer each time water is poured over them and last several months before dissolving. When starting a new liquid fertilizing routine on a new bonsai, cut the recommended concentration in half and monitor before making any adjustments. Apply during the spring, summer, and autumn months. For beginners, a balanced fertilizer will do, one that has a nitrogen, phosphorus, and potassium (**NPK**) ratio of three similar numbers, such as 5:5:5.

WINTER CARE

Transitioning from autumn to winter can be harsh on indoor bonsai and they will need time to adjust to the change in temperatures. Be watchful when heaters start turning on, and monitor how quickly planters are drying out by checking their soil, or picking them up and feeling their weight. A hygrometer is useful to check indoor humidity levels; if it frequently drops below 35%, a humidifier or a small tray containing water and rocks helps increase moisture levels. Another great way to combat dry air is more plants! More plants mean more moisture in the air. Note that many bonsai will shed leaves when getting accustomed to winter 'indoor' conditions and 20-30% leaf loss is not uncommon. Less light in winter can also prove challenging. If your plant needs more, try a grow light to extend daylight by a few hours. Find a high-quality full spectrum grow light - cheaper grow lamps using blue/red LED diodes are not as effective.

For outdoor plants, check nightly temperatures are within a suitable range. Most outdoor plants can take freezing temperatures and snow, but sustained winds and extreme cold could cause dieback. Protecting the root system is most important: bury the pot in a layer of mulch, or place inside a separate container that drains, adding mulch around the base. For mild protection from northerly winds, place inside a box with an open side facing south for air and light; this is especially important if your bonsai are on a terrace or rooftop. Make sure plants can access rainwater or snow melt and, if there has been no moisture for several weeks, supplement by watering occasionally. In extremely cold environments, with consistent freezing temperatures, an unheated wooden shed or outdoor structure would make an acceptable home.

COMMON PROBLEMS

WATERING
Aside from regular watering, there are certain times of year where watering problems occur more often. Pay attention to extreme temperature and humidity changes during the hottest and coldest months, when dry air and heat will pull moisture from the plant at a faster rate. Both times of year can also coincide with going on holiday: if you need to leave for an extended period, find a responsible plant-sitter! If you forgot to water and think your tree is in trouble, water right away. If the root system is still healthy it may recover, but expect the leaves to turn pale and drop off. It may take weeks to months for the tree to put out any new growth, but if the branches are still pliable then parts of it may still be alive. Check to see if the tips break off easily. If the branches snap, it is likely too late. Overwatering can also cause similar distress signals. Most bonsai do not like consistently soggy soils, and yellowing leaves could be a sign you are not allowing enough time for the root systems to breathe. Make absolutely sure your planter has drainage holes, so water is not pooling in the pot.

PESTS
Bonsai have tiny but persistent enemies. The main culprits will be aphids, scale insects, spider mites, mealy bugs, and fungus gnats. Inspect your plants weekly for any signs of pests, checking under leaves where they often like to hide. Keep your plants clean and tidy; remove fallen leaves and soil spills when they occur. Sap-sucking aphids often appear in spring and summer. Look for them grouped

together on new growth tips and under leaves. At the same time, ants might appear. Ants will not harm the plants but they should be kept away as they are a vector for aphids and mealy bugs. Some pests complete their life cycle in the soil, like fungus gnats. Proper elimination is knowing how to target pests various stages. For example, employing the use of soil-based nematodes that hunt down the larvae can effectively stop gnats from turning into adult flies. For large plant collections we recommend spraying pre-emptively every few weeks with an organic pesticide, such as neem oil mixed with a small amount of plant-based washing up liquid. If you have a serious infestation, look to stronger formulas like pyrethrin, following the manufacturer's instructions for application. Pests often hitch a ride on a new plant. When sourcing, ask if your plant has had any problems recently. If you are buying from a professional seller, and one who really cares about their plants, they will give you a clear answer about in-house treatment schedules and methods. In case you bring home a bargain-bin plant, or one you couldn't resist rescuing from a bin, be very scrutinizing, and consider quarantining before introducing it to the rest of your plant family. It can be a long hard fight to get rid of a recurring pest problem, so be vigilant and research your enemy. For a deeper discussion into pests and disease, there are many published resources that specifically cover them in greater detail.

FUNGUS/MOULD

White mould or powdery mildew can affect the leaves and the top soil of plants when there is lack of good air circulation. Make sure the room in which you have your bonsai is well ventilated; proper air circulation helps the overall health of plants. When you cannot leave the windows open use a fan to keep the air moving, or place your bonsai in an area where human activity generates air movement! Any exposed area of the plant or top layer of soil that stays consistently damp may be an attractor for mould spores. Treat the area by manually removing the mould with a pick or bonsai tweezers, and let it dry out more frequently.

LEAF SPOTS AND BLOTS

It is natural for older leaves to weather and fall off eventually, but if more than 50% of your indoor bonsai tree is losing its leaves rapidly it could be due to sudden changes in temperature, insufficient moisture, or lack of good drainage. Mineral deficiencies could also be causing leaf discolouration. Lack of phosphorus or potassium could be causing leaves to turn yellow, but this can be remedied by applying fertilizer.

INDOOR BONSAI

The bonsai in this section are categorized as Indoor in most temperate zones in Europe, North America, and Asia, but in subtropical or tropical zones many of them can live quite well outside. Check the temperature requirements before buying.

BARBADOS CHERRY TREE

MALPHIGIA PUNICIFOLIA

Whoever thought bonsai couldn't be delicious didn't try growing *Malphigia punicifolia*. This Caribbean native was once relatively unknown until it exploded in popularity because of its cherry-like fruit called acerola, which are rich in Vitamin C and are now grown commercially to be used in health foods and juices. To get fruits on a bonsai, you may need to cross-pollinate with more than one plant.

⚘ Elliptical leaves grow on sturdy branches that can get quite large. When blooming, prune away larger leaves that might hide clusters of small pink flowers.

☀ Full to partial sun.

◊ Keep moderately moist throughout the year, provide extra humidity in winter.

° Keep between 4°C (40°F) and 38°C (100°F). To bloom, will need warm, humid temperatures.

⠿ Adaptable to most soils, if well drained. Provide a mix of 60% grit and 40% organic matter.

🪰 Watch for aphids, which like to attack leaves in late spring.

WIANDI FICUS

FICUS BENJAMINA 'WIANDI'

Native to Southeast Asia and the Caribbean, this 'Wiandi' cultivar has curly branches that support a dense canopy of elliptical shiny green leaves. It can take shadier conditions than most other banyans. **CAUTION:** Watch out for the sticky white sap that emerges from wounded leaves and branches; it contains latex and could be an irritant.

✤ This naturally falls into a weeping form once branches are long enough. Be careful when cleaning or styling branches that have hardened, as they break off easily. Thin out the branches that start to cross each other to fully enjoy the distinctive curves.

☀ Partial light to shade. Can adjust to full sun if given time to acclimatize.

◊ Water well during spring and summer, when new growth is emerging. Cut back watering in winter to when the surface starts to feel slightly dry. Thicker leaves help it to withstand the drier conditions of winter easier than many other types of indoor bonsai.

° Maintain a steady temperature between 10°C (50°F) and 32°C (90°F). Rapid temperature changes will lead to leaf drop, as will reduced light levels in autumn and winter.

▦ Use a mix of 65% coarse sand and 35% organic matter. Repotting can be done successfully with care at most times of the year.

🪲 Watch out for scale insects and mealy bugs.

BALD CYPRESS

TAXODIUM DISTICHUM

This deciduous conifer is one of the largest trees native to the southeastern United States. Often seen lurking in swamps covered with moss, *Taxodium distichum* are mysterious and intoxicating – locally they are often called 'swamp totems'. Soft needle-like leaves are sage green in the summer, turning pumpkin brown in autumn or winter. In the wild, submerged roots – commonly known as 'cypress knees' – tend to protrude from the soil surface. When mature, this plant will have small brown cones about 2.5cm (1in) across.

✂ Bald Cypress can be trained for formal upright styles easily or can be pruned into pyramidal shapes. Leave the bottom third of the trunk free of branches to visually elongate the height of the tree. Keeping branches clipped will encourage dense growth closer to the trunk.

☀ Full sun, or bright indirect light.

○ Water abundantly during the growing season.

° Tolerant of light frost, but keep between 2°C (35°F) and 38°C (100°F). If kept indoors in winter, keep in a cool, humid environment to induce a dormant resting period, and provide good air circulation.

⠿ Well adapted to wet or salty soils, but as a bonsai will fare better in free-draining humus-rich soils. Use 65% grit and 35% organic matter.

🪲 Watch out for mealy bugs and spider mites.

FICUS TOO LITTLE

FICUS BENJAMINA 'TOO LITTLE'

Another cultivar of *Ficus benjamina* but less pendulous, with an upright growth pattern and smaller leaves. It has a forgiving nature and fun styling opportunities, so is a good choice for any beginner bonsai collection. It adapts well to indoor conditions, even the heat of dry winter environments.

CAUTION: Watch out for the sticky white sap that emerges from wounded leaves and branches; it contains latex and could be an irritant.

✂ Keep the trunk free from too many tightly-packed branches to allow better light and airflow to the core. This will encourage better growth and allow the trunk to thicken faster.

❋ Full or partial sun, to bright shade.

◐ Keep damp but not soggy throughout the year. Has good drought tolerance so water when the surface is slightly dry. Spray or mist to increase humidity and encourage aerial roots.

° Keep between 7°C (45°F) and 32°C (90°F).

⁙ Use a mixture of 65% coarse sand and 35% organic matter with fine particles sifted out. Repotting can be done successfully with care at most times of the year.

🐞 Prone to mealy bugs, scale insects, and spider mites.

BOUGAINVILLEA

BOUGAINVILLEA SPECTABILIS

This climbing deciduous shrub is a fast-growing flowering plant native to Brazil. When blooming it produces clusters of pink tissue-papery bracts in hues of pink and scarlet, which recall images of this plant happily growing against the sunny stucco walls of Mediterranean climes.

✂ Large branches can be pruned in late winter. Flowers are born on new growth, so allow it to grow freely and prune until after flowering.

✷ Full sun – if possible, a southern-facing window with full morning sun and bright afternoon sun will provide the right light levels. If placed outdoors in summer, give it full morning light.

◊ Can survive dry spells and a bit of neglect. Regulate soil moisture to avoid it becoming too soggy or bone dry. In winter allow to dry out until the leaves droop before watering; this will encourage flowering.

° Keep between 7°C (45°F) and 38°C (100°F) in a well-ventilated area. Cooler temperatures of between 10°C (50°F) and 15°C (60°F) in winter will allow it to store the energy required for flowering.

⦂ Use a soil mix of 70% organic matter, sifting out any fine particles, and 30% grit such as coarse sand or crushed stone. Needs to drain well, especially in winter.

🪰 Watch for aphids or whitefly.

SEA GRAPE

COCCOLOBA UVIFERA

This sun seeker native to the Caribbean is usually found near the sea, and is distinguishable for its round leathery leaves that catch and deflect the light at different angles. New leaves start out slightly curled with a reddish tint. When older, if given the right conditions, leaf veins will darken to a deep red in a striking contrast to the green leaves. As the name suggests, its grape-like fruits are edible, but it will rarely fruit when kept indoors as a bonsai.

CAUTION: Leaves of the Sea Grape are used to being battered and beaten and it is normal if they show signs of wear by summer's end.

- ✄ This is all about those large round leaves and a lot of territory can be covered with them. Style for a pleasing profile so that even when backlit or seen from afar, it will command a sculptural presence. Large leaves can be cut in half to encourage new growth, or removed altogether.

- ☀ Full sun. Strong sun will help it develop darker reds in the leaves.

- ⬤ Keep soil moderately wet without getting soggy. If it is slow to drain, check the drainage.

- ° Best between 10°C (50°F) and 38°C (100°F).

- ⠿ Prefers well-drained sandy mixes, but tolerant of many soils. Aim for a mix of 70% grit and 30% organic matter.

ELEPHANT BUSH

PORTULACARIA AFRA

In its native South Africa, this succulent shrub can grow to several feet high and is on the menu for elephants – when trampled the broken pieces easily propagate into new plants. Given enough light, it is a top recommendation for beginners due to its ease of care. The leaves of the variegated variety have cream-coloured edges.

✂ Wiring can be done to younger branches but check and rewire as necessary because they thicken quickly. Unless training a new branch, cut back new shoots to 2.5cm (1in) to 5cm (2in), leaving one to three leaf pairs. These leaf pairs will frequently split and create two new shoots, and growth can be directed by choosing which to leave. Pruning can be done any time during the growing season.

☀ Full sun year round. Some shade is tolerable for short periods but will get leggy and lose leaves if not given enough light.

◊ Water regularly in summer when kept in full sun, waiting until the soil surface is very dry. Cut back watering in autumn and winter; wait until the leaves start to get slightly soft and crinkly.

° Between 4°C (40°F) and 38°C (100°F). Can be taken outside in summer if placed to get morning sun or indirect afternoon sun; this strengthens branches and will produce more growth.

⁞⁞ 70% fine gravel and lava rock provides good drainage; the remaining 30% can be compost or other organic matter.

SALTWOOD

NEEA BUXIFOLIA

The Saltwood is native to Puerto Rico and surrounding islands, where it grows on semi-exposed ridge tops. It is an evergreen with small leaves and compact branches, reddish in colour when young, which it sends out in all directions. In spring it produces small, light yellow, bell-shaped flowers. The trunk is usually a washed grey in colour and develops a thick root flare, adding to the mature look.

� Lots of dense branches will create a heavy foliage that needs to be pruned back, and erratic shoots can be hard to wire. Work with the natural growth pattern to create groupings with a strong profile, similar to a topiary.

☀ Partial sun with some light shade tolerance. In winter, it will need bright light or will lose many leaves.

◊ Does not like to dry out completely. Keep soil damp throughout the year and water when the surface is dry to the touch.

° Keep above 4°C (40°F). Heat hardy up to 35°C (95°F). Does best in well aerated environments.

⁞⁞ Use a quick-draining soil with at least 35% coarse sand and 65% organic matter. Can be repotted any time of year.

WILLOW LEAF FIG

FICUS NERIIFOLIA

Native to the Himalayas and southern China, where it can grow up to 15m (50ft). The leaves are pointed and elongated, resembling those of the willow. Although quite messy, shedding leaves any time conditions change, it is a hardy tree and recovers from leaf loss to put out new growth when stabilized.

CAUTION: Like most ficus, will ooze a milky sap that should be wiped off any tools.

✂ Prune during the growing season, cutting the longest new shoots back to five or fewer leaves. Choose an outline to maintain to guide the shape; broom-style bonsai is common to this tree. Wiring can be done on branches two to three years old.

✳ Likes full morning sun or partial afternoon sun. A change in light conditions usually sets off a yellowing and dropping of leaves.

💧 Water regularly during the growing season, cutting back in winter or if it has dropped more than 20% of its leaves. In winter, increase humidity to encourage leaf buds.

° Fluctuating temperatures can lead to leaf drop. Keep above 4°C (40°F) and below 35°C (95°F).

⠿ 65% quick draining fired clay or grit, and 35% rich organic matter. Cuttings are easy to propagate.

🪲 Check for spider mites and mealy bugs, which can hide among the branch nodes where it can be difficult to spray.

DWARF UMBRELLA TREE

SCHEFFLERA ARBORICOLA 'LUSEANE'

The leaves of the *Schefflera arboricola* are a glossy green and fan
out like tiny umbrellas, or small exploding fireworks. It is a popular
bonsai choice due to its low-light tolerance and easy care. In nature
it is sometimes epiphytic, growing on other trees and capturing water
from the air. It is native to Taiwan, part of this country's small but
diverse flora.

CAUTION: This is not a pet-friendly tree because it is toxic to animals.

- Keep the trunk visible by removing excess leaves around the base. If
  the tree is growing too quickly, remove the tip of the leading branches
  to slow it down and promote lower growth.

- Partial sun or bright indirect light. Although tolerant of low light,
  will become susceptible to water damage so will require monitoring.

- Allow the surface of the soil to dry before watering as it does not like
  consistently soggy soil. Adjust watering to the light conditions; in a
  shady spot, it will use less water. Darkening and burning at leaf tips
  could be a sign it is overwatered or staying too wet. Make sure the
  leaves are properly dried and avoid misting too often.

- Keep in temperatures between 10°C (50°F) and 35°C (95°F).

- Use a rich organic soil that drains well; 65% coarse sand or grit
  and 35% organic matter with fine particles sifted out.

- Susceptible to spider mites, mealy bugs, aphids, and scale insects.

JABUTICABA

PLINIA CAULIFLORA

In its native Brazil, the Jabuticaba is distinguishable for the many grape-like fruits that grow directly on the trunks and branches. Nutritional and sweet, they're eaten raw like grapes, or used to make a variety of sauces and drinks. As bonsai, this makes a fine tree due to its graceful and smooth trunk, and ability to adapt to a variety of soil conditions. New leaves are tinged in pink and older bark will exfoliate to reveal cream colours.

✂ Trim branches once during and after the growing season to maintain shape. A slow-growing tree and easy to wire, a good styling option would be slanted, formal, or informal upright.

☀ Full sun, bright indirect light, or light shade.

◊ Keep consistently moist through the growing season, cutting back slightly in winter.

° Best between 4°C (40°F) and 35°C (95°F).

⦂ Prefers deep, rich organic soils that drain well, but will adapt to sandy soils given enough moisture. Use a combination of 60% grit and 40% organic matter.

EUROPEAN OLIVE

OLEA EUROPAEA

A symbol of peace since ancient times, *Olea europaea* is a Mediterranean native with oblong leaves that have a silvery sheen to help protect the leaves from the harsh sun. The fruit is famously used for its oil, and the plant is resilient, long-lived, and also makes a fine bonsai. The heavily marked trunk naturally twists when older, while simultaneously turning lighter and softer.

✝ Scars and marks on the trunk add to the weathered look of this tree, a nod to the gnarly olive trees of the Mediterranean. Use a knob cutter when removing a branch close to the trunk; the pockmark will scar over and look like the branch had fallen off naturally.

❋ Olives need plenty of sun and are heat tolerant once they have a developed root system.

◐ Drought tolerant when established.

° Best between 4°C (40°F) and 38°C (100°F). In winter, keep below 21°C (70°F). Can survive freezing temperatures for short periods, but try to keep above 0°C (32°F) or add protection in winter. Can successfully be placed in an unheated greenhouse, shed, or garage in winter provided it has natural light.

⋮⋮ Make sure your soil mix has good drainage by adding small stones or lava rock. A mix of 30% organic and 70% inorganic is a good rule.

🪲 Watch for scale and spider mites, spraying immediately if you see anything.

MING ARALIA

POLYSCIAS FRUTICOSA

The finely segmented feathery leaves of the Ming Aralia make it a good shade tree, especially where one might need it under the hot sun of its native India. It is a popular choice for indoor areas that don't get a lot of direct sunlight, and the tall and compact profile make it an attractive bonsai for narrow spaces. To accentuate the height and improve airflow to the roots, elevate the planter on a small trivet or bonsai stand.

✂ Its growth habit is vertical and, as the tree grows, lower leaves will die off and expose corky bark. An ideal look is a thick trunk with many sets of closely-jointed branches and a dense canopy of leaves. Prune tips of new growth to redistribute more energy into the trunk.

☀ Partial sun to light shade. The soft light of full morning sun is best.

◊ Maintain consistent moisture in spring and summer, but do not overwater. Cut back watering in winter; increase humidity and water only when the soil surface feels dry.

° Keep between 10°C (50°F) and 32°C (90°F).

⦂⦂ Use a mix with 40% organic matter and 60% fast draining grit. Repot in the spring only when roots have become sufficiently constricted.

BLOODWOOD

HAEMATOXYLUM CAMPECHIANUM

This Mexican and Central American native is a member of the legume family and has heart-shaped leaves and fragrant yellow flowers. It is commonly called bloodwood after the distinctly red heartwood that 'bleeds' when cut; it was once used commercially as a textile dye and became an important replacement for the more expensive indigo.

✂ Wire branches within a few years, before hardening off, and have fun with styling the leaves to highlight their hanging nature. When pendulous they catch air currents to create added movement. New shoots are vigorous growers and should not get longer than 15cm (6in) before they are pruned back.

❋ Full to partial sun. In summer provide light protection during the hottest part of the day.

◊ Keep well watered during the growing season; an abundance of leaves will quickly transpire the soil moisture. In winter keep damp and water when the soil surface feels dry; the thin leaves dry out quickly in dry winter environments. A humidifier nearby or a humidity tray under it will help.

° Keep between 10°C (50°F) and 35°C (95°F). Needs a warm and humid environment year round.

⁘ Prefers a humus-rich soil with proper drainage. Use a mix of 60% coarse sand or lava rock and 40% organic matter.

HARLAND BOXWOOD

BUXUS HARLANDII

This dense rounded shrub is native to China and Southeast Asia. It grows elongated leaves from deeply fissured branches and trunk. In spring it produces small, greenish-yellow blossoms, which are attractive to bees but ornamentally lacklustre. Although fine indoors it should not be placed next to a heat source and needs good air circulation.

✄ Cut back new shoots to 2.5cm (1in) or less in early summer. Shaping can take on different styles, such as formal/informal, upright and slanted. Wire young branches before hardening off, in about three to four years, and be sure to remove wire before it digs into the bark. The furrowed bark complements deadwood sculpting well.

☀ Does best in a bright sunny spot with full morning or afternoon sun.

◊ In summer water frequently. In winter only water when the surface feels dry to the touch, but never allow to completely dry out.

° Cold hardy down to minus 1°C (30°F), and heat hardy up to 35°C (95°F). Benefits from a seasonal rest so should be kept between 7°C (45°F) and 15°C (60°F) in winter. Place in an unheated room or cold window bay with a fan or ventilator in the room for air circulation.

⠿ A mix of 70% coarse sand and calcined clay and 30% organic matter. Keep soil from getting acidic by limiting peat in the mix.

🪲 Watch out for scale insects, caterpillar moth, and box blight.

PREMNA

PREMNA SPECIES

Premna is native to the Indian subcontinent and Southeast Asia. Small leaves and a beautifully textured trunk make this a great bonsai option, given enough light and humidity. A vigorous grower, it can put out many shoots in summer that quickly get to 30cm (12in) or longer.

✂ If the leaves are getting too large, move to an area with more sunlight. Leaf prune larger leaves that cast too much shade to encourage smaller leaf growth. The branches and trunk will develop character with little wiring, and this plant accommodates driftwood styles. It will take to frequent pruning throughout the year; cut back the new shoots to two or three leaf pairs several times during the growing season.

❋ Full sun to bright partial sun. An eastern-facing window is good.

◊ Water well in spring and summer during the growing season. Do not let dry out and maintain a humidity level above 35% in winter.

° Do not allow to drop below 10°C (50°F). Keep away from strong heaters in winter; add a room fan to circulate the air if it's too still.

⁝⁝ A well-drained mix of 65% grit and 35% organic matter. Fertilizing will encourage flower buds.

🪰 Look out for spider mites and spray at the first sign of cobwebs – hold a piece of dark paper behind the leaves to see them better. Spray well where nodes and leaves are dense and could provide a hiding place.

SERISSA

SERISSA JAPONICA

Populating open woodlands and wet meadows in Southeast Asia, this flowering semi-evergreen is beloved for the white flowers that bloom throughout the year; it's nicknamed 'Tree of a Thousand Stars'. **CAUTION:** For those who want a challenge, Serissas are notoriously unpredictable, and lose leaves or entire branches without warning when there is a change in growing conditions. When trying to recover they often suffer from too much care, when they would rather be left alone; gradual changes are always best.

✀ Exposing the roots in a technique called neage fits this species well. Another popular styling method is root over rock, where the roots hang over and hug a boulder. Wiring and pruning can be done throughout the year, but preferably after the growing season and not after repotting.

☀ Partial or full sun throughout the year.

◊ Water well throughout the year but avoid soggy soil. A humidifier or tray of water will help maintain ambient moisture levels. Will be very thirsty during the heavy part of the growing season.

° Keep between 13°C (55°F) and 38°C (100°F). Sudden changes in temperature may induce leaf drop, so keep at a steady temperature if it is already performing well. Good ventilation helps this plant.

⁞⁞ Use a mix of 80% organic matter and 20% coarse sand or fast-draining calcined clay.

PINK LILIAN POWDERPUFF

CALLIANDRA BREVIPES 'PINK LILIAN'

This evergreen perennial shrub is a rare species native to Brazil, and is characterized by delicate small leaves aligned in rows. When flowering, expect pink puffy flowers and lots of covetous stares from friends.

✄ It is beautiful to see this tree totally covered in leaves and let it go wild, but it looks best when kept light and airy by keeping growth in check. Cut branch tips before they get too long and make sure they don't start crowding the trunk. Prune in late spring to control the rapid growth of new shoots, and again after blooming.

☀ Direct to indirect sun. When full of leaves and bushy, protect from the full heat of the midday sun.

◊ A thirsty plant in spring and summer, so water accordingly. Leaves will turn yellow and shed rigorously if the plant is stressed as a result of drought. If the problem is rectified quickly it will recover; watch for new leaves to appear in four to five weeks and clear off any dead leaves.

° Maintain between 10°C (50°F) and 35°C (95°F). Likes humid, warm environments and will benefit from misting when the air is below 40% humidity.

⁞⁞ Use a fertile soil that retains moisture and stays evenly wet. Aim for a mix of 60% organic and 40% free-draining grit. Apply a general fertilizer in spring and summer.

BRAZILIAN RAINTREE

PITHECELLOBIUM TORTUM

Few bonsai have the ability to express their condition so quickly and playfully as *Pithecellobium tortum*. When disturbed or agitated long enough, they respond by folding their compound leaves together – and at night they might even appear to be 'sleeping.' The light and airy green leaves are gentle enough to rock in the slightest movement of air, such as when one walks by.

CAUTION: Be aware of sharp thorns, which are especially hard when growing near the trunk.

✂ Easy to prune and shape, with plenty of leaves to create foliage mounds, so many shaping styles work well. Is most often seen as a formal or informal upright or broom style. Control the burst of summer growth by pinching back the terminal bud of the new leaf tips. This will encourage branch ramification and denser growth lower on the branch.

☀ Full or bright indirect light. If placed in full midday sun, provide some protection on summer afternoons by pulling away from the window.

◊ Keep well watered in spring and summer. In winter, the thin leaves benefit from additional humidity by occasional spraying. Do not allow to dry out too much or it will defoliate.

° Keep between 7°C (45°F) and 32°C (90°F). In winter leaves will not dry out as much if kept between 13°C (55°F) and 18°C (65°F).

⁛ A mix of 60% organic matter and 40% coarse sand or other grit.

MOUJEAN TEA

NASHIA INAGUENSIS

The leaves of this plant are so fragrant that they can be recognized from a distance and are sometimes used in teas for their citrous-vanilla scent. It is native to the Caribbean islands where it can be seen growing naturally in rocky outcroppings. Small fragrant white flowers appear in clusters along the stem in summer to autumn.

⚑ Will tend to form extra roots at the base of the trunk, making it a good candidate for the neagari style of bonsai where the top roots are exposed. When repotting, remove some soil near the root flare and plant a little higher to achieve the effect. Prune back new shoots to control the amount of transpiration in summer and be careful when wiring due to the fragile branches, which are similar to rosemary in structure.

☀ Situate in a bright spot with full or partial sun. Leaves may suddenly brown and mould over due to lack of sun or poor ventilation.

◊ This is a thirsty plant. Water well during spring and summer, cutting back slightly when temperatures start to drop. Never allow to dry out or it will quickly suffer dieback. Keep humidity above 40% in winter.

° Keep between 10°C (50°F) and 35°C (95°F) and give plenty of good air circulation. Will need warmer temperatures to bloom.

⁝⁝ Use a quick-draining soil that holds some moisture between waterings. Aim for a mix of 70% grit and 30% organic material.

🐞 Watch out for fungal and bacterial leaf spot.

GOLLUM JADE

CRASSULA OVATA 'GOLLUM'

A succulent shrub hailing from South Africa and Mozambique, *Crassula ovata* has many cultivars including this one with its trumpet-shaped leaves that end in a fluted tip. In the right conditions the leaves turn pink or red, and it grows a well-developed trunk that supports the weight of thick fleshy leaves. This succulent shrub is a top recommendation for beginners for its ease of care and quirky looks.

✂ Heavy clumps of leaves at the end of branches may weaken the branch or weigh it down too much, so clip off areas to lighten the weight. These can be planted to create new plants.

☀ Full sun is best, but if unavoidable some shade won't kill this plant.

◊ Wait until the soil has become very dry then water fully and deeply, giving every area of the planter time to soak up moisture. It is better to underwater than overwater, as consistently wet roots will start to rot. Some people wait until the leaves become slightly wrinkled before watering.

° Will easily take temperatures up to 38°C (100°F), but keep above 4°C (40°F).

⣿ A well-draining mix consisting mostly of coarse sand and lava rock or baked clay will help keep roots from staying wet for too long. Keep organic matter to 30% or less of the total composition.

NATAL PLUM

CARISSA MACROCARPA

Carissa macrocarpa is a semi-tropical evergreen and native coastal dweller from South Africa, where its glossy oval leaves and edible red berries – called *noem-noem* in Afrikaans – reflect the sun's rays. When raised as bonsai and brought to eye level, the seasoned look of the trunk becomes a point of natural beauty, too.

CAUTION: All parts except the fruit are poisonous to pets. Also, be careful of the spines when handling.

🌱 New shoots, if left alone, will quickly increase the height of the plant. Depending on the location within the crown, and the ultimate height it is to attain, prune back to 7.5cm (3in) or less. The remaining leaf pair below the cut will often create two new branches. Thin out some leaves to avoid branches becoming too dense and heavy.

☀ Full sun to partial shade.

💧 Moderate watering throughout the year. Water when the soil starts to feel dry, but do not allow to completely dry out.

° Provide good airflow, and temperatures between 10°C (50°F) and 29°C (85°F). Good airflow is important in winter via a nearby fan.

⁙ Needs a well-draining soil, 70% sand, lava rock, or fired clay and 30% organic matter.

🐞 Watch for spider mites, which like to hide under the slightly cupped leaves. Remember to spray under the leaves when treating.

PHILIPPINE TEA TREE

CARMONA MICROPHYLLA

Carmona microphylla is native to Southeast Asia and at home in warm humid climes. It bears tiny white flowers that bloom throughout the year, followed by green berries. The compact size of the leaves make this tree look proportionally balanced even when young. Another common variety, *Carmona macrophylla*, has longer, wider leaves and will fill out a larger area.

✂ Showcase the naturally gnarly trunk by keeping the base of the trunk visible and prune off any shoots that appear near the root flare. Pruning can be done throughout the year as necessary.

❋ Full morning sun, or bright indirect afternoon sun. Intense afternoon sun will stress the plant if it is not receiving enough moisture.

◊ This can be a thirsty plant, especially after new growth. Keep soil fairly wet in spring and summer, and reduce in winter. Keep humidity levels high by placing a tray of water nearby, or with a room humidifier.

° A steady 21°C (70°F) to 29°C (85°F) will encourage flowering. Do not let temperatures fall below 10°C (50°F). Warm temperatures up to 38°C (100°F) are fine if the tree has enough water.

⁝⁝ Use a free-draining mix that will not become waterlogged: 50% coarse organic matter, free of small particles, and 50% inorganic.

🪰 Aphids like to attack new growth; treat with an insecticide or a simple horticultural oil and soap solution.

LAVENDER STAR FLOWER

GREWIA CAFFRA

This native to Australia and southern Africa is often grown as a garden shrub and rises to popularity every spring, when lavender star-shaped flowers appear near the tips of its branches. They seem large for such a small plant, but in the windy habitats where they grow a large landing strip might be necessary for pollinating insects. If given the right conditions it may bloom during other times of the year.

✂ Focus on controlling the stumbling, branching habit when pruning back in spring. Prune to one or two leaf pairs, then let it put out new branches on which it will bear flowers in late spring and summer. Some control of these long shoots will be needed after flowering or they will take all the energy of the plant and continue elongating.

❉ Bright indirect light throughout the day works best, but can acclimate to full sun or light shade.

◊ Needs moderate moisture. Wait until the surface is slightly dry to the touch and then water without allowing the soil to become waterlogged.

° Keep between 13°C (55°F) and 26°C (80°F).

⋮⋮ A mix of 65% organic matter to 35% coarse sand or other grit is best.

CHINESE BANYAN

FICUS MICROCARPA

A hardy indoor bonsai, and a beginner favourite, the glossy green leaves of *Ficus microcarpa* adorn branches that drop suspended aerial roots and can eventually become columns of support for the growing canopy. Native in densely shaded and damp jungles over a wide area spanning the Indian subcontinent to southeast Asia, China, and Australia. **CAUTION:** Watch out for the sticky white sap that emerges from wounded leaves and branches; it contains latex and could be an irritant. Any cuts to large branches should be sealed with bonsai cut paste.

✂ Pruning may need to be done several times a year when this is growing rapidly. Aerial roots can be directed to areas of the planter that draw the eye back down to the trunk and suggest expansion.

☀ Partial sun or light shade; can tolerate a range of light conditions.

◊ Water well in spring and summer at the first sign of new growth, cutting back in winter; water when the soil is dry to the touch. Has some drought hardiness when developed and forgives a missed round of watering. Increased humidity helps encourage aerial root growth.

° Maintain a steady temperature of 10°C (50°F) to 32°C (90°F). Rapid changes in temperature will lead to some leaf drop.

⁛ Use a mix of 65% coarse sand and 35% organic material with fine particles sifted out. Repot with care at most times of the year.

🪲 Watch out for mealy bugs, scale insects, and spider mites.

BUDDHIST PINE

PODOCARPUS MACROPHYLLUS

One of the few indoor bonsai with needle-like leaves, *Podocarpus macrophyllus* is a handsome evergreen with a stable trunk that supports clouds of green foliage. It is often found in temple grounds and gardens around its native China and Japan, leading to its common name.

✂ Trim to direct energy where you want the tree to grow fastest. New shoots can be easily trained to form curvilinear shapes. Pruning can be done at any time of year. Leaves just below a cut will hide the wound and help recovery, so avoid cutting these.

☀ Partial sun, but can adjust to lower light levels. Keep away from hot afternoon sun in summer, which could burn new leaf tips.

◊ Keep well watered during the growing season but cut back in winter. Pale or brown-tipped leaves are a sign it's too dry. Do not let the humidity drop below 30% or leaves could desiccate and turn brown. Do not fertilize after autumn to slow the growth in winter.

° Keep between 4°C (40°F) and 38°C (100°F). Best above 10°C (50°F), avoiding sharp changes of temperature.

⦂ Use a well-drained soil mix of 60% organic matter and 40% inorganic. When repotting, do not remove too many roots from the shallow root system.

🐞 Watch out for aphids, mealy bugs, and scale insects.

GREEN ISLAND FIG

FICUS MICROCARPA 'GREEN ISLAND'

For a rugged, easy-care, and slow-growing bonsai, the Green Island Fig is not lacking in imagination or adventure. Its branches tend to spread sideways, dipping slightly before swooping upward, and often bear fruits that resemble mini figs. Watch for aerial roots that will mysteriously twist their way around the trunk and base to form a dense root buttress. CAUTION: Will emit a sticky white sap that can be an irritant and will also gum up your tools if not cleaned off.

⚘ Channel what comes to mind when hearing 'green island'; train to grow wider than taller, with a slight pyramidal centre. Give yourself additional points for a branch that hangs near the edge of the planter, and any sandy shores. Can be pruned at any time of the year. Cut back new growth to four leaves or less to maintain the shape.

☀ Place in direct to partial sun. Adapts to low light conditions but may lose foliage density.

◊ Water regularly in summer, keeping the soil evenly moist without becoming soggy. In winter, don't allow to dry out completely. High humidity will encourage formation of aerial roots.

° Keep between 7°C (45°F) and 32°C (90°F).

⁂ Repotting can be done any time of year, with a mixture of 65% coarse sand and 35% organically rich material.

🪲 Prone to scale insects, mealy bugs, and spider mites.

DWARF BLACK OLIVE

BUCIDA SPINOSA

Also known as the Dwarf Geometry Tree, this is native to the Florida
Keys, Cuba, and the Caribbean. It has a branching pattern that fans
out, with compact leaves on spiny geometric branches and tiny cream-
coloured flowers. In the wild, it can grow to 12-15m (40-50ft). It will drop
some leaves, though not all, throughout the year; new leaves are bronze
coloured before turning green, and turn red or orange before dropping.
New growth regenerates quickly in the right conditions.
CAUTION: Watch out for spines when handling.

⚓ Branches have a natural geometric pattern that should be highlighted
when seen from above or below. Wire any branches to bring them into
a lateral position and create strong layered tiers along the height of
the main trunk. A leading branch will grow straight up, taking a lot of
energy with it; cut it unless you want height added quickly.

☀ Full sun to partial sun; a south-facing window is best.

◊ Keep evenly damp during the growing season and do not allow to dry
out in winter - a humidifier will help. Leaves can suddenly desiccate
and curl if humidity drops or during sudden changes in environment;
remove dried leaves and increase humidity to 40% or more.

° Maintain in a steady temperature between 10°C (50°F) and
32°C (90°F).

⋮⋮ Repot in summer in a mix of 65% grit and 35% organic matter.

BELL MIMOSA

DICHROSTACHYS CINEREA

A native to Africa and India, this plant provides a durable hardwood used for great walking sticks and other domestic items. It has a wide variety of other traditional uses and provides nutrients for numerous animals and insects. It has fine leaves on leggy branches, and the dramatic flowers hang like pink and yellow pendants.

↬ The tall and leggy nature makes this suitable for literati style bonsai, where they mimic the growth of a tall solitary tree in the distance. Prune out new rapidly growing shoots in spring and again in mid-summer. Prune to favour crooked vertical branches that support layers of foliage in the canopy where the sun hits.

❊ Needs full sun or bright indirect sun. On the hottest summer days leaves can fold up to protect from water loss.

◊ Keep damp throughout the year, but don't let it sit in water for any extended time as it prefers to dry out a little. If it has put out a lot of new growth, water more often until pruned back.

° Keep between 7°C (45°F) and 38°C (100°F). Good air circulation via a room fan or open window will help keep the trunk healthy.

⁛ Provide a mix of 70% inorganic and 30% organic. Soil must drain quickly or should be changed. Repot when root bound about every three to four years; take a moment to appreciate the strong earthy scent of the roots when repotting.

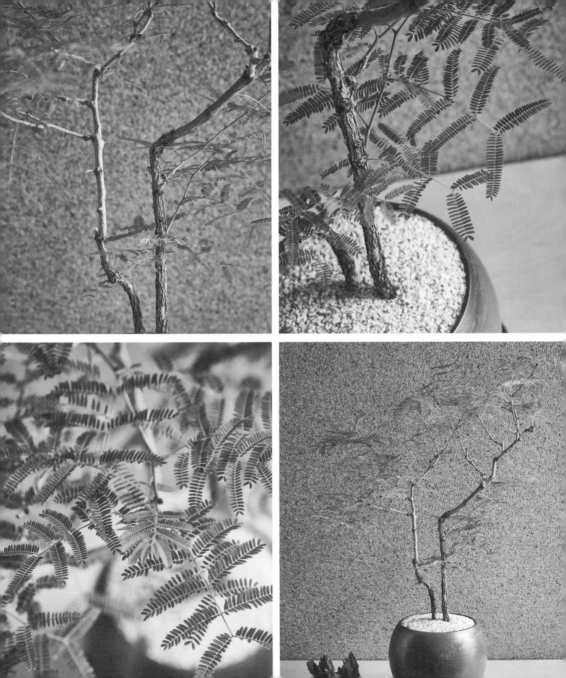

CHINESE ELM

ULMUS PARVIFLOLIA

From street tree to indoor bonsai, the adaptable Chinese Elm can be seen growing in almost every form and size, with fine-toothed leaves adorning graceful lines. Forgiving of mistakes, and fast growing, it is considered one of the most reliable and beginner-friendly bonsai.

✂ Easy to wire and adapts to most bonsai styles. Pruning is often all that is needed to maintain shape. Pinch back vigorous new growth to two or three leaves in spring to summer. Rapidly growing shoots can be stopped by pinching off the terminal bud at the desired length.

☀ Full or partial sun, but give some protection from very hot afternoon sun – especially in summer. Expect some leaves to be shed in autumn as an adaptation to changing light levels and humidity.

◊ Water well during growth spurts, especially in summer. Allow soil surface to dry out between waterings in winter, but keep a room humidifier or tray of water nearby.

° Keep between 4°C (40°F) and 35°C (95°F). Does well when kept slightly cooler in winter, around 15°C (60°F).

⠿ Use a mix of 60% organic and 40% fast-draining coarse sand. Repot every few years when slightly pot-bound.

🐞 Aphids, whitefly, and spider mites like to attack this tree; any sudden defoliation could be a sign of infestation. Remove infected areas and spray all areas with an appropriate insecticide. If caught in time it will quickly rebound as soon as signs of danger are removed.

OUTDOOR BONSAI

The bonsai in this section are categorized as Outdoor in most temperate zones in Europe, North America, and Asia. In subtropical and tropical zones many of them will do poorly outside because they need the cold temperature of winter. Check the temperature requirements before buying.

HORSFORD CONTORTED CANADIAN HEMLOCK

TSUGA CANADENSIS 'HORSFORD CONTORTED'

This narrow-leafed evergreen is native to the eastern United States and Canada, where it's often seen on slopes and mountainous areas. This particular cultivar has branches that twist and coil, naturally forming a contorted shape. In spring the leaf buds are covered in chestnut coloured fuzzy hairs. The bark of the Canadian Hemlock contains tannins, traditionally used for tanning leather and clothes, and it has a mildly sweet forest scent when pruned or repotted.

✂ Control new growth from spring to autumn by pinching out new buds, being careful not to break the needles. Wiring can be done, but styling is often done through pruning alone. Take advantage of the unique growth habit by letting some branches hang. Visually it looks better if branches are not allowed to cross.

☀ Full sun to part shade, needs protection from hot sun in summer.

💧 Although drought tolerant, it will lose leaves during long dry periods. Maintain steady moisture, especially on very hot days and in dry winters. Water more in spring and summer.

° Cold hardy to minus 12°C (10°F) but may need protection from strong winter winds. Keep below 38°C (100°F) in summer.

⁙ Use a rich well-draining soil of 60% organic matter and 40% grit.

BEARBERRY COTONEASTER

COTONEASTER DAMMERI 'STREIB'S FINDLING'

This small semi-deciduous bush that is native to central China puts on a year-round show, forming small white blooms in spring followed by berries in late summer that turn red in winter, and colourful leaves in autumn. Cotoneasters are traditionally used as ground cover for their low, quickly spreading habit. They provide a lot of activity to interest an eager bonsai collector.

CAUTION: Resist the temptation to bring indoors for winter, even for a short time, as dry indoor air will quickly desiccate the leaves.

- ✄ Can be trained for cascading bonsai styles by leaving some of the lateral and hanging branches. This plant likes to spread quickly and will put out new shoots from its root system. Unless you want a multi-stemmed look, prune away the ground shoots closest to the base of the trunk or it will get messy fast.

- ☀ Full to partial sun. They can adapt to shade, but may not bloom or fruit as abundantly.

- ○ Water well during spring and summer.

- ° Keep between minus 1°C (30°F) and 35°C (95°F).

- ⁘ Not picky with soil, as long as they have good drainage, and easy to repot. Use a mix of 50% fast-draining grit and 50% organic matter.

CHIRIMEN HINOKI CYPRESS

CHAMAECYPARIS OBTUSA 'CHIRIMEN'

Native to Japan, this *Chamaecyparis obtusa* cultivar is unique for its upright bluish-green shoots that grow in tightly-packed irregular clusters, becoming a natural sculpture all on its own. Clumps of seed cones in spring may look like deformities along the trunk, but these are normal and will fall off. The cultivar name refers to a type of crepe fabric that has a wrinkled texture.

✂ The formal, upright bonsai style fits this tree. Wire carefully so as to not trap any foliage and prune in spring and summer. You'll want to save clippings and sprinkle them in the bathroom or shower for the great scent.

❋ Full to partial sun but is tolerant of some shade. Provide protection on very hot sunny days

◊ Keep moderately moist in a well-drained soil. In dry winters, water so that the soil never gets bone dry.

° Best between minus 6°C (20°F) and 38°C (100°F). Protect from strong winter winds or cover with a light layer of sacking (burlap) if temperature gets very cold for more than a week.

⣿ A mix of 60% organic and 40% coarse sand or lava rock. Slow growing, but can be repotted every two to five years.

LITTLE JOHN HINOKI CYPRESS

CHAMAECYPARIS OBTUSA 'LITTLE JOHN'

This compact evergreen tree is native to Japan and has tight sprays of gently curling leaves that evoke the image of water falling. The leaves have a sweet scent when rubbed, prompting many admirers to 'pet' this tree. Tannins in the wood help prevent rot – making the Hinoki Cypress a common material seen at temples and baths.

✢ Some leaves experience natural dieback every year, especially those close to the trunk and in the core; clean them out regularly by twisting the dead leaf and breaking off where leaf sections connect. Thin the dense core to encourage more light and air. This tree looks great styled as a double trunk. Prune to feature the compact fans and accentuate the falling water look, as this is one of its best characteristics.

☀ Full sun or partial-shade. May need protection from strong winter winds.

◊ Maintain a high level of moisture in spring and summer to encourage growth. In winter, water when the surface of the soil starts to feel slightly dry. Beware tip blight can affect the leaves in consistently wet weather.

° Keep above minus 6°C (20°F). In winter protect from blustery winds and shade from full sun on any unusually warm days.

⁞⁞⁞ A mix of 60% organic and 40% coarse sand or lava rock. Repot in spring before new growth emerges.

LACEBARK ELM

ULMUS PARVIFLORA 'SEIJU'

This compact deciduous tree with small elliptical leaves is a native to eastern Asia. The serrated leaves will display some yellow colour in autumn and with age the corky bark exposes browns and creamy greys after flaking. Lacebark elms backbud just about everywhere, including the lower trunk, and are prolific in producing new shoots after pruning or wiring, making them a fun bonsai to learn and train with.

✂ The exfoliating bark is stunning and should be featured on this tree. The wood stays pliable for several years and can be wired, but remember to cut the wire off before it damages and marks the trunk. Pinch prune throughout the growing season; major pruning can be done in late winter or early spring.

☀ Full sun, with some protection in summer from harsh afternoon sun.

○ Water regularly and never allow to get dry in spring and summer when new growth appears. Keep evenly moist but not soggy in winter.

° Keep between minus 1°C (30°F) and 32°C (90°F). Although cold hardy, find a protected spot in winter away from prolonged cold winds that can kill younger branches.

⁞⁞ Does well with a 60% organic and 40% inorganic composition, but adaptable to many soil conditions.

DWARF MOUNTAIN PINE

PINUS MUGO 'VALLEY CUSHION'

This bushy evergreen has small needles, which have a refreshing pine forest scent when crushed that transports you to its native habitat: the mountains of central Europe. Whereas height can vary among mugo pines, 'Valley Cushion' is a true dwarf variety with a height of 30cm (12in) or less. Its small but playful nature works well when placed in areas that the eye might casually fall, like the entrance gate post to a small garden, or just beyond a bathroom window.

✂ Dwarf varieties used in bonsai usually grow wider than taller, giving a toadstool look. Pruning can be done in spring after candles have formed, although some people prefer to let it go for several years before styling. Slow-growing branches will stay pliable for years.

☀ Full or partial sun is preferred.

💧 Water regularly in spring and summer when new candles are forming. In winter, water enough to keep the soil from completely drying out if there is no natural precipitation.

° Cold hardy down to minus 17°C (1°F), but only for short periods. Keep below 38°C (100°F) in summer.

⁞ Use a free-draining soil, with at least 70% grit. Repotting can be done every five to eight years if the tree is healthy.

DWARF ALBERTA SPRUCE

PICEA GLAUCA CONICA 'HUMPTY DUMPTY'

This small conifer was first discovered in Canada and has light green needles with a fresh scent. Relatives in the northern forests of North America often get up to 15m (50ft) in the wild, but this is a naturally dwarf variety. Slightly pyramidal due to its width, and very slow growing, it develops a thick trunk comparable to its height.

✀ Densely packed needles means the inner core can get very dark. Clean out the older dead needles throughout the year, which will increase the airflow and light to the core.

☀ Full to partial sun, but tolerant of some shade. If too sunny in summer, place in a bright but protected area. Make sure you provide good air circulation; if too close to other trees or in a stale environment will suffer foliage and branch dieback in patches.

◊ Water to keep evenly moist throughout the year, allowing to drain properly each time.

° Keep between minus 12°C (10°F) and 29°C (85°F). Cold hardy but will struggle in hot and humid environments.

⁞⁞ A well-draining mix of 70% organic matter and 30% coarse sand. When repotting do not remove all the beneficial mycorrhizae, which surround the roots and look like dry white mould; it forms a symbiotic relationship with the tree.

AMERICAN HORNBEAM

CARPINUS CAROLINIANA

This deciduous tree, which is native to lowland forests of the eastern United States, is sometimes called Musclewood due to its sinewy twisted trunk. The leaves have a soft gleam and straight side veins with finely toothed edges. Autumn colours range from lemon yellow to coffee brown. Branches slightly zigzag and droop as they get longer.

✂ Thin the branches to increase airflow to the core; their unique shape lets them flutter in the wind when given enough room to breathe. Prune out older dead branches in winter and keep new shoots to a minimum of three leaves in spring and summer, thinning out any larger leaves that block too much sunlight.

☀ Partial sun to bright indirect light. Shading the roots and planter to keep them cool will mimic the environment to which they are naturally adapted.

◊ Water abundantly in spring and summer as soon as new leaves start to emerge. Water less in winter but maintain consistent moisture without letting the soil totally dry out.

° Keep between minus 6°C (20°F) and 38°C (100°F). Periods of freezing are tolerable, but extended lengths of very cold and windy conditions will cause dieback.

⁙ Use a mix of 50% organic and 50% fast-draining coarse sand. Hornbeams grow in moist rich soils near ravines in lowland forests.

SHIMPAKU JUNIPER

JUNIPERUS CHINENSIS 'SHIMPAKU'

In its natural habitat in the mountains of Japan, this is a gnarled windswept evergreen that bears the scars of years of growth and dieback. Naturally low in form, it provides a lot of styling and creative opportunities. Sometimes the bark is purposefully removed to expose the white heartwood, adding age and character to an already beautiful tree.

- ✂ This is a popular choice for jin- and shari- style pruning. Use sharp tools and jin pliers to peel off sections, leaving strips of bark on the branches that will be kept alive or else you will kill all the foliage. Pruning and wiring can be done at any time of the year, common styles are windswept and slanted.

- ☀ Full sun to partial sun.

- ◊ Keep medium moist but not waterlogged. Water well in spring and summer and frequently when under the full summer sun.

- ° Best between minus 6°C (20°F) and 32°C (90°F) but will tolerate colder temperatures for short periods. Do not keep under minus 6°C (20°F) for prolonged periods or foliage discolouration might occur.

- ⠿ Use a soil mix that drains well, 20% organic and 80% hard particles and coarse grit. A slow-release balanced fertilizer can be applied from spring to autumn.

- 🪲 Watch for spider mites and prone to fungal problems, especially if not kept in a sunny, well-ventilated environment.

BOXWOOD

BUXUS SPECIES

Once often used in traditional garden landscapes as border hedges and foundation plantings, this ubiquitous shrub can be appreciated in a whole new way through bonsai training. The hard, slightly fissured bark can be styled like driftwood and will age handsomely, a quality lost when the plant is boxed in with dense growth. Mostly appreciated for its evergreen quality; small spring flowers and autumn colour is undistinguished, but adds to seasonal interest.

✂ Can be treated like a block of marble. Start with overgrown stock and prune away branches to reveal a more characterful shape. Older branches are too stiff to wire alone, so cut away dense younger shoots to create room. Can be shaped and heavily pruned regularly.

✳ Full morning sun, or partial afternoon sun. Some shade during the hottest parts of summer will help avoid stress.

◊ Water just enough to keep damp throughout the year.

° Keep between minus 6°C (20°F) and 38°C (100°F). Able to withstand even colder temperatures, but will need protection from severe cold and wind or will suffer leaf discolouration or dieback: lightly wrap with sacking (burlap) or place behind a wind screen.

⁞⁞ Repot in spring every few years with a soil mix of 70% organic matter and 30% free-draining coarse sand. If soil is not draining well enough, leaves may lose their green colour.

🪲 Prone to scale insects.

DWARF BIRCH

BETULA NANA

This deciduous dwarf shrub with small round-toothed leaves is native to the arctic regions of Canada and Europe. In the wild it forms a bush about 1.2m (4ft) tall, and as a bonsai can be trained to a comfortable 60cm (2ft) or less. In winter the cute glossy leaves turn an unspectacular yellow and brown before defoliating.

⚹ Young, tender shoots tend to die off in blistery winters and must be pruned out in spring. This tree likes to spread, and new shoots will appear near the base, befitting a twin or triple trunk bonsai arrangement. These can be encouraged to fuse with the trunk to create the image of much larger multi-trunked birches seen at the edge of meadows.

❋ Full sun to light shade. On hot summer days place in bright light away from direct sun.

◊ Water well in spring and summer. Water less in winter but do not allow to dry out completely.

° Keep between minus 17°C (1°F) and 29°C (85°F). Can take very cold temperatures in winter but does not like very hot days in summer.

⸬ Will tolerate either wet or fast-draining bonsai soils. Use a mix containing at least 30% organic matter.

JAPANESE HOLLY

ILEX CRENATA 'DWARF PAGODA'

This is a compact evergreen shrub with emerald green leaves that are slightly cup shaped and tightly stacked. It grows to 60cm (2ft) or less. White flowers in spring are not ornamentally showy, but it may produce globular green and black fruits in summer.

✣ Expect growth of about 2.5-5cm (1-2in) per year, which can be shaped and pruned frequently. A natural irregular branching structure welcomes shaping through pruning alone, and removing crowded branches that all emerge from the same trunk area will create room to separate and appreciate the dense leafy clusters.

✺ Adaptable to a wide range of light conditions, from full sun to full shade. When in full summer sun, keep the planter from getting too hot or it might roast the roots.

◊ Water well in spring and autumn and keep moderately moist in winter.

° Keep between 0°C (32°F) and 32°C (90°F). Protection from strong winter winds that can desiccate the leaves is important, especially if there is a winter drought. Consider spraying the leaves with an anti-transpirant according to directions if proper protection can't be provided.

⁝⁝ Likes a quick-draining acidic soil with added pine needles or fir bark. Aim for 60% organic and 40% inorganic.

CREPE MYRTLE

LAGERSTROEMIA INDICA

There's little not to like about *Lagerstroemia indica*, with its true representation of changing seasons. In summer colourful flowers emerge, ranging from pink to lilac. In autumn expect a flaunting show of oranges, reds, and yellows, sometimes all on the same branch. Even when bare of its leaves in winter, the bark patterns remain colourful. It is native to India and southeast and east Asia.

✆ Bring attention to the trunk line by encouraging some height. Underplant with small grasses or ferns to draw attention to the root flare, which will be the first area to show flaking and mottled bark. Do any heavy pruning in autumn. In late spring, prune back new growth to several leaf nodes.

☀ Full or partial sun.

◊ Water well in summer when it transpires a lot, do not allow soil to get bone dry. Maintain moisture in winter – supplement if there is winter drought.

° Keep cool in the winter but not freezing. To maintain dormancy in winter temperatures should not climb above 13°C (55°F) for long. In summer, 38°C (100°F) is the upper limit – provide some shade if temperatures reach that high.

⁛ Use a mix of 60% organic and 40% inorganic.

🪰 Prone to powdery mildew so keep well ventilated. Watch for pests in summer; if you see ants on the trunk, look for tiny aphids near any new leaves.

ABBOTT'S PYGMY CANADIAN HEMLOCK

TSUGA CANADENSIS 'ABBOTT'S PYGMY'

This cultivar was discovered in Vermont and is one of the smallest and slowest growing hemlocks. Fortunately it is not the same type of hemlock that poisoned Socrates so don't be afraid to get close, as the soft needles and compact branching are best viewed at eye level. **CAUTION:** Sometimes a branch will die leaving a hole in the canopy. Prune out the dead material and allow light to penetrate the core. If given enough light, older branches will form new leaf buds.

✁ Take advantage of the tight growth pattern and prune into grouped sections, thinning out crowded branches in the interior to increase airflow. As this grows very slowly at the top, keep several lower branches open and visible for a balanced vertical transition.

❋ Full sun to light shade, needs some protection from hot summer sun.

◊ Keep moderately moist all year without letting it get too soggy or too dry. If the roots are tightly packed, the planter will hold less water. In this case, water deeply and thoroughly.

° Keep between minus 12°C (10°F) and 35°C (95°F). Watch out for harsh temperatures and water well during any heatwaves.

⁞⁞ Use a mix of 60% free-draining soil and 40% organic matter with fine particles sifted out.

BOYD'S DWARF WILLOW

SALIX BOYDII

A slow-growing deciduous shrub first discovered in the exposed highlands of Scotland, where conditions forced it to grow among rocky outcroppings. Like many other willows it will sprout fuzzy catkins in spring, which unfurl into slightly dimpled leaves that open by summer. Small hairs further protect the leaves from the elements (like a tiny little coat). These cute and furry leaves turn sickly yellow and brown in autumn before falling off in winter, leaving the plant bare until spring.

⚲ Naturally branches to a handsome form without much crowding, but will need to be pruned in the first few years as smaller shoots die back. Shoots can easily be trained into lots of bonsai styles within the first few years when pliable. Leaves like to grow at the ends of branches, so encourage groupings of leaves at different height intervals by keeping a varied spread.

☀ Full sun or some partial sun.

◊ Water thoroughly and frequently, especially during the hot summer months and after the leaves unfurl.

° Cold hardy to minus 6°C (20°F). Protect younger shoots from frost and freezing winds or significant dieback will occur.

⣿ Use a fast-draining soil that retains some moisture; 60% grit and 40% organic matter.

JAPANESE WHITE PINE

PINUS PARVIFLORA 'AOI'

The Japanese White Pine is a classic variety of pine with a long history of bonsai cultivation in its native Japan and Korea. This is because of its styling opportunities and mixture of 'soft' and 'hard' energy, which is partly due to having softer needles than the rigid Black Pine.

✄ Prune out the new growth, called candles, in summer when they reach 5-7.5cm (2-3in) by removing the top half. Large branch pruning can be done in autumn or late winter. Takes well to wiring and any wounds to the bark will soon add to its sturdy presence. Remove any dried needles throughout the year to keep tidy and airy. An upright informal or slanting style fits well with its natural growth habit.

☀ Full or partial sun for optimal health.

◊ Water well in spring and summer but keep well drained throughout the year. If there is no winter precipitation for over two weeks, water to prevent from drying out.

° Keep between minus 6°C (20°F) and 38°C (100°F). As with most needled evergreens, only bring inside to display for a few days at most, and never in winter. At night place back outdoors.

⁞ Repotting can be done in spring. Use a mix high in free-draining components, such as 80% lava rock or akadama, with 20% moisture-retaining compost or peat. If roots are tightly wound, cut the lower quarter to open up the root ball.

NORWAY SPRUCE

PICEA ABIES 'LITTLE GEM'

This mountain-dwelling evergreen native to northern and central Europe is known for its bun-like shape and tight grouping of needles. Grown in the wild it makes an excellent timber tree when big, but this dwarf variety will stay shorter than 60cm (2ft). Low branching and a thick lower trunk are a plus on this tree, making it look older and bigger in less time.

✂ High density in the core will lead to dieback and lack of air flow, which *Picea abies* desperately needs. Prune out the core from unwanted overcrowding and create spaces between the branches so visually it is easier to read. Hard pruning can be done in the autumn, and new shoots can be controlled in the spring after the first flush of growth. Seasonal dieback of needles should be pulled and cleaned off throughout the year.

☀ Full to partial sun. In winter, watch out for unusually warm days and place in the shade to keep from overheating.

💧 Water well starting in spring through summer, do not let dry out in summer. Reduce watering when the weather starts to cool off.

° Keep between minus 17°C (1°F) and 26°C (80°F). Spruce are very cold hardy, but must be kept below 10°C (50°F) in winter to stay dormant.

⁝ Keep well drained in a mix of 70% organic matter and 30% coarse sand. Repotting can be done in late winter or spring, but leave some soil as there are often beneficial mycorrhizal fungi helping the root system take up nutrients.

JAPANESE GARDEN JUNIPER

JUNIPERUS PROCUMBENS 'NANA'

The hardiness of Japanese garden junipers, paired with their natural droop, have helped them become a popular bonsai, available at garden centres and even many florists. They ship well, repot easily, and are tolerant of lightweight sandy soils. When cared for properly, the spiny-pointed needles have a blue to silvery-green colour.

- ⚘ *Juniperus procumbens* will easily take to a cascade or semi-cascade style. Often very low to the ground, so prune any underside needles to create more space for the trunk and neat lines. Pruning can be done any time of year.

- ☀ Full or partial sun.

- ⬤ Water well in spring and summer, cutting back in autumn and winter. Has drought tolerance when established but should never get completely dry.

- ° Keep between minus 6°C (20°F) and 38°C (100°F). Often mislabelled as indoor bonsai, they tend to suffer in dry, hot environments in winter, and are best kept outside.

- ⣿ Use a well-draining mix of 40% organic matter and 60% inorganic.

THOWEIL HINOKI CYPRESS

CHAMAECYPARIS OBTUSA 'THOWEIL'

Chamaecyparis obtusa is native to the mountainous areas of central Japan. Full and upright, this slow-growing evergreen has naturally sculpted irregular branches covered in scale-like leaves that form fanned out tips. When crushed, the foliage releases a lemony scent.

⚘ This variety naturally grows upright and columnar, but the trunk remains fairly flexible for several years and can be wired into informal asymmetric shapes. Tips can be pinched back as necessary throughout the year, major branch pruning should be done in summer.

☀ Full morning or early afternoon sun. Full summer sun can dry the planter out quickly so some protection might be needed.

◊ Water well in spring and summer when new growth appears at the tips. Soil should never become dry, even in winter. Foliage and branch dieback can occur if some areas of the root system are not being watered enough.

° Keep between minus 6°C (20°F) and 32°C (90°F). Will tolerate very cold conditions but protect from winter wind.

⁖ Soil should be well draining but hold consistent moisture without becoming soggy and compacted. Use a mixture of 60% loamy rich soil and 40% inorganic grit.

HEAVENLY BAMBOO

NANDINA DOMESTICA

Not a true bamboo, but heavenly nonetheless, *Nandina domestica* is a durable semi-deciduous shrub native to China and Japan. Various shades of red and green appear in cooler months, browning late in winter if temperatures are very cold. In spring watch for new stems, bearing three light green leaves. Can be used as a symbolic substitute for bamboo to add interest to a collection.

✂ Thin out older branches that die off, and remove young shoots damaged by frost. Planting mature stalks with younger ones will make a suitable forest group planting. *Nandina* spreads by putting out new shoots around the base of the trunk. If creating forest plantings, have a separate grow pot as a nursery, from which you can collect new shoots.

☀ Will adapt to full sun or shade. In high summer, protect slightly from burning midday sun.

💧 Water regularly in summer, especially if in full sun. Keep wet but not waterlogged throughout the year.

° Best between 4°C (40°F) and 38°C (100°F). Will withstand some frost but could lose some smaller branches. To maintain dormancy in winter, temperatures should not climb above 13°C (55°F) for long.

⋮⋮ This tree likes fertile soils. Use a 70% organic and 30% coarse sand mixture, sift out finer particles and be careful the mix does not clog the drainage hole or repotting will be needed right away.

🪲 Relatively pest free but will attract powdery mildew if not kept in well aerated conditions.

JAPANESE MAPLE

ACER PALMATUM 'RHODE ISLAND RED'

A small, mountain-loving tree prized for its elegance and stunning and colourful display; it retains a deep red colour throughout summer and becomes warm yellow, bright orange, or fiery red in autumn. It is a pleasant sight in spring when small baby maple leaves begin to emerge and slowly unfurl. The leaves hold on through November, but will get tattered at their tips and can be removed at their base.

✣ Maples can be styled in many ways due to their pliable branches when young. When pruning the branch tips, notice which direction the next set of leaf buds points, and remember that they may become the next set of growth. You can direct growth by leaving the leaf buds in areas you want to encourage.

❋ Full and filtered sunlight. Provide protection from harsh afternoon sun in summer or leaves can become sunscorched.

◊ Keep evenly moist during spring and summer. In winter only water when there has been no rain or snow for over two weeks, or on unusually warm or sunny days.

° Keep between minus 4°C (25°F) and 32°C (90°F). Will withstand periods of freezing weather, but blustery days can damage branches. In severe cold, place in an unheated shed or garage.

⁝⁝ Use a mix with good drainage that will not stay soggy wet. Prefers organically rich soil so use a mix of 40% organic matter and 60% fast-draining grit. Repot when the roots are slightly pot-bound.

akadama - a natural granular material mined from volcanic soil. It retains water and nutrients but also offers good drainage. It darkens when wet, providing a visual indication of when the plant needs more water.

animist - the belief that all objects, places and creatures have a spiritual essence and can be considered as alive.

backbud - this is when buds closer to the trunk are activated to grow instead of those at the tip of the branch. Backbudding can be activated on some bonsai by hard pruning.

bracts - a modified leaf that can be larger and more colourful than a genuine flower.

broom style - a straight and upright trunk that finishes in spreading branches forming a rounded shape. The Japanese name for this style is *hokidachi*.

calcined clay - clay that has been fired; it looks like fine gravel but will hold water and nutrients without becoming waterlogged.

candles - when referring to conifers, new shoots from which new needles emerge.

cascade style - a tree that grows bending downwards, which is hard to achieve because it is opposite to its natural tendency to grow upwards. This sometimes occurs in nature on trees hanging at the edge of cliffs. The cascade bonsai often extends below the bottom of the pot so is displayed on a stand to allow room. The Japanese name for this style is *kengai*. With a semi-cascade style the downward direction is not so defined; the tree grows downwards but not below the bottom of the pot and also sideways to extend beyond the side of the pot. The Japanese name for this style is *han-kengai*.

dieback - when branches or leaves die from their tip backwards towards the main plant. It can be caused by disease or an unfavourable environment.

driftwood style - very similar to shari style, but a larger area of the tree is bare of bark and branches, with just narrow strips of living wood to support the growing areas.

forest planting - a style of bonsai that includes several of the same type of tree growing in a grouping.

epiphytic - a plant that grows on another plant, depending on it for support but not for sustenance.

jin style - the technique of removing bark from the branches so the bare living wood beneath is revealed. Often done in conjunction with shari.

literati style - mimics the look of a solitary tall tree in the distance, with a tall bare trunk that is sometimes crooked rather than straight, finishing with branches only at the top. This shape often occurs in nature when the tree is surrounded by other nearby trees and has to compete for sunlight.

neagari style - or exposed root style; the top roots are exposed so the tree looks as if it is sitting high.

NPK ratio - nitrogen, phosphorus, and potassium ratio in a fertilizer.

pot-bound - when the roots form a compact ball that fills the pot, leaving no room for further growth.

root over rock style - in which the roots hang over and hug a rock, reaching down in search of nutrients. The Japanese name for this style is *seki-joju*.

shari style - the technique of removing bark from the trunk. In nature some trees lose bark over quite large areas due to harsh weather conditions. For bonsai styling it is removed in a band along the trunk, that grows gradually narrower up the tree. The bare wood is then bleached to imitate the action of the sun.

Shintó - the traditional religion of Japan.

slanted style - in this style the tree leans in one direction at an angle of about 60 degrees, as if growing towards the sun or constantly subject to strong winds. The branches should be wider on the side away from the lean to balance the overall look of the tree. The Japanese name for this style is *shakan*.

symbiotic - a relationship between two different organisms that benefits both.

transpire - giving off water vapour.

upright style - this can be formal or informal. In the formal upright style, the trunk is straight and tapers from thick at the base to thinner towards the top. The branches begin about a quarter of the way up the tree, with a single branch at the top. The Japanese name for this style is *chokkan*. With the informal style, the trunk curves in an 'S' shape with a branch at each turn. The Japanese name for this style is *moyogi*.

windswept style - in nature this happens when a tree is continually blown in one direction by strong winds. The trunk bends in one direction and, although the branches grow all around it, they will eventually all be bent in the direction of the trunk, which makes this different to the slanted style. The Japanese name for this style is *fukinagashi*.

SUPPLIERS

US SUPPLIERS

Bonsai Empire
Starter kits, plants, courses
bonsaiempire.com

Bonsai Jack
Soil, supplies, pots
bonsaijack.com

Bonsai Mirai
Classes, supplies, pots
bonsaimirai.com

Allshapes Bonsai & Nursery
Plants, pots, soil, tools, courses
allshapesbonsai.com

Gardino Nursery
Plants
gardinonursery.com

Wigert's Bonsai
Plants, pots, soil, tools, courses
wigertsbonsai.com

UK SUPPLIERS

Banksia Bonsai Nursery
Plants, pots, soil, tools, courses
bonsaitrees.uk.com

Greenwood Bonsai Studio
Plants, pots, soil, tools, courses
bonsai.co.uk

Heron's Bonsai
Plants, pots, soil, tools, courses
herons.co.uk

Wattston Bonsai
Plants, pots, soil, tools, courses
wattstonbonsai.com

Windybank Bonsai
Plants, pots, soil, tools
windybankbonsai.co.uk

JAPAN SUPPLIERS

Kaneshin Bonsai Tools
Tools – ships worldwide
kaneshin.shop2.multilingualcart.com

ABOUT THE AUTHOR

Matthew Puntigam studied garden design and bonsai in Japan before returning to New York City to pursue a masters in Landscape Design. He started growing bonsai outside his window on a small fire escape, finding the interaction with trees to be indispensable for city living. In 2016, he founded Dandy Farmer to introduce the art of bonsai to others, with the mission of bringing plant care into everyone's daily routine. He is excited to see interest grow as more people take up this art form to express themselves, while also rediscovering nature at an instinctive level.

dandyfarmer.com

ACKNOWLEDGEMENTS

Thank you to all the plant parents, creatives, and network of supporters who have been near and far on this journey and from whom I continually learn. Special thanks to the teams at Sinajina Bonsai and Kuge Crafts of Tokyo Japan, who were instrumental in setting me on this path, and to family members who never discouraged me from getting dirty in the woods. A big thank you to Paul and his tireless dedication to my bonsai narrative.

PUBLISHING DIRECTOR Sarah Lavelle
SENIOR COMMISSIONING EDITOR Harriet Butt
SERIES DESIGNER Gemma Hayden
JUNIOR DESIGNER Alicia House
PHOTOGRAPHER Jonathan Hökklo
HEAD OF PRODUCTION Stephen Lang
PRODUCTION CONTROLLER Sinead Hering

Published in 2021 by Quadrille,
an imprint of Hardie Grant Publishing

Quadrille
52-54 Southwark Street
London SE1 1UN
quadrille.com

Cataloguing in Publication Data: a catalogue record for this book
is available from the British Library.

Text © Matthew Puntigam 2021
Photography © Jonathan Hökklo 2021
Design and layout © Quadrille 2021

ISBN 978 1 78713 647 2

Printed in China

FSC
www.fsc.org
MIX
Paper from
responsible sources
FSC™ C020056